HUNTERDON

A Celebration of Communities

To Kathleen

2006

Enjoy the beauty of Hunterdon

...especially Clinton!

Walter Choroszewski

WALTER CHOROSZEWSKI

Published by

AESTHETIC PRESS, INC.

North Branch, New Jersey

HUNTERDON, *A Celebration of Communities*

ISBN: 1-932803-45-9
First Printing - 2006
Printed in Korea

AESTHETIC PRESS, INC.
P.O. Box 5306, North Branch, NJ 08876-1303

Website: www.aestheticpress.com
Email: info@aestheticpress.com
Telephone: 908 369-3777

HUNTERDON
A Celebration of Communities

WALTER CHOROSZEWSKI

▲ *Califon*

◀◀ *East Amwell*

HUNTERDON

FOREWORD *by*

WALTER CHOROSZEWSKI

I 've never seen the rolling green pastures of County Ayr in Scotland, covered with spotted dairy cattle, but I have discovered similar bucolic scenes in the fields of the Amwell Valley.

I imagine that, almost three hundred years ago, Robert Hunter may have found a familiar comfort in the fields and pastures of this Western-Division of New Jersey. Ayrshire, on the southwestern coast of Scotland, was home to "Hunterston"—the old-world family home and namesake of Hunterdon County, which was created by Robert Hunter, the 4th royal governor of New Jersey.

Under the rule of Queen Anne, New Jersey became a Royal Colony in 1702, reuniting Proprietary East Jersey and West Jersey. The first royal governor of this new territory was Edward Hyde (Lord Cornbury), an ineffective ruler known for his corruption.

Hyde was replaced by John Lovelace in 1708, who served as governor for both New York and New Jersey. Lovelace was able to convict a number of Cornbury's associates, but died in office in May 1709 and was replaced by the lieutenant governor of New York and New Jersey, Richard Ingoldesby.

As acting governor, Ingoldesby was the subject of suspicion by the proprietors of New Jersey. A few years earlier, Ingoldesby was an enemy of Cornbury. Now in office, he seemed as equally corrupt as Cornbury, with his attempt to divert funds meant for Lovelace. His commission was revoked less than 6 months after taking office, but he served until the following spring when word of his dismissal finally reached him.

In 1710, General Robert Hunter was appointed the new royal governor of New York and New Jersey with a mandate to clean-up the corruption and settle the disputes between the quarreling proprietors. Hunter succeeded in his mission and also was effective in making other reforms in the courts. He is perhaps best known for establishing a new county.

After residents of West Jersey had petitioned the colony to alleviate their hardship in traveling the great distances to the county seat in Burlington, an act was passed on March 11, 1713 forming a new division called "The County of Hunterdon."

Old Hunterdon was much larger than Hunterdon County today, extending from the Assunpink Creek near Trenton north to the border of New York State, and included today's Morris, Warren, Sussex and Mercer counties. In 1752, when England and all its possessions converted from the Julian to the Gregorian calendar, Hunterdon County's date of formation was revised to March 22, 1714.

Just as Hunterdon may have evoked memories of home for Robert Hunter, Hunterdon also reminds me of my childhood home in northeastern Pennsylvania. I find similarities in the rural landscape and friendly people —helping me to recall simpler times of the 1950s and 1960s.

Although I now live in neighboring Somerset County, I consider Hunterdon to be part of my Central Jersey home. When my family and I moved from New York to New Jersey in the mid-1980s we hoped to settle in Hunterdon County. The 1980s real estate boom was just beginning and for various reasons, our attempts to purchase property in Tewksbury, Readington and Califon didn't work out.

My love affair with Hunterdon began in 1980 when I was photographing New Jersey for my first book. I recall driving through Sergeantsville in search of the last covered bridge of the state and marveling at the farm vistas along Route 604 near Rosemont. I continued along the rocky Wickecheoke, stopping by the mills at Prallsville. I passed through quaint Stockton, then south along the Delaware River to discover the galleries and antique shops of Lambertville.

After settling into our New Jersey home, side trips to Hunterdon were more frequent and I continued to photograph and feature the county in my books and calendars. In 1998 I published **LAMBERTVILLE**— a small book which celebrated the 150th anniversary of this quaint river town. **HUNTERDON COUNTY, A Millennial Portrait**, was published the following year and featured the scenic beauty of the county at the turn of the new century. In the spring of 2006, I approached the Hunterdon Medical Center Foundation with the idea of using a new book on the county as a fund-raiser. This new title, **HUNTERDON, A Celebration of Communities,** offers a photographic essay of each of the county's 26 municipalities.

Although a few of the images were photographed in previous years, photography for this project began in earnest during the fall of 2005. The cover image was shot from the bridge near First and Main in Califon on Halloween in the warm afternoon sun. A half-hour later, while driving down Route 513, I pulled over to shoot a telephoto view of the sunlit houses along Taylor Street in High Bridge. Winter followed and with each fresh snowfall I returned to Hunterdon in search of pristine seasonal views.

Color returned in the spring with lime green leaves and white and pink blossoms. It also ushered in a new season of lambs, calves, crias (baby alpacas) and foals. I loved discovering and photographing the many animals of Hunterdon—both domestic and wild. In fact, this book contains over 200 photos of birds and beasts in Hunterdon.

Of all the animals, I think the horse is the most closely associated with Hunterdon County. I photographed horses at the Chamber of Commerce event "Hunterdon Horse Expo," I captured the competitive Driving Event at the Delaware Valley Horsemen's Association and thrilled at the equestrian jumps at Briarwood Farm. I stopped to visit the "retired" horses at Fawn Run Farm in East Amwell and photographed one curious mare as she came over to the fence to greet me and *take a bite* from the nearby flower bed. Most of all, I appreciate the majestic beauty of Hunterdon's equine population as they grace the fields of almost every township.

In addition to shooting my favorite rural landscapes, this project gave me the opportunity to attend and photograph numerous events held throughout Hunterdon County. Each week I would review the local newspapers for a list of parades, fairs and festivals and map a route to visit as many as possible. From the patriotic 4th of July Parade in Lebanon to the fashionable "Pooch Parade" in High Bridge; from the Blueberry Festival at the Stanton Community Grange, to the Hunterdon County 4-H & Agricultural Fair at the new county fairgrounds in East Amwell; from Lambertville's 25th annual Shad Fest to the visually spectacular New Jersey Festival of Ballooning at Solberg Airport in Readington.

The people of Hunterdon are generous and they support many worthy causes. I attended numerous fund-raising events like the South Branch

Watershed's "Ride for the River" (starting from Spruce Run State Park), as well as the Tewksbury Education Foundation's 11th Annual Barn Dance and Auction where the second grade quilt fetched an astounding $4,000!

Dining in Hunterdon County is always a treat for my wife, Susan, and me. We enjoyed Susan's birthday lunch at Craig Shelton's incomparable Ryland Inn, our anniversary dinner at the elegant Stockton Inn and scrumptious French Toast on a sunny Sunday morning outside Mark Koppe's General Store in Bloomsbury.

Writers and artists have always been drawn by the muses of Hunterdon. In 1714 Hunterdon's patron, Royal Governor Robert Hunter, was the first published playwright in America with his political satire, **Androboros**. The Hunterdon Museum of Art in Clinton offers classes and exhibits and the galleries of the river towns showcase many local artists. Toshiko Takaezu creates her clay vessels in Franklin, while David Rago and Suzanne Perrault auction fine arts and antiques in Lambertville. Children's book author Laura T. Barnes writes about her "Barnesyard" animal friends in Sergeantsville, and the Chris Val Band brings country music to the Kingwood Fire House every Saturday night and is broadcast on WDVR-FM's "Heartlands Hayride."

Country music and general stores are still present in a county that has not yet been homogenized to look like every other locale in New Jersey. Hunterdon prides itself on preserving the past, including protecting its precious farmland as well as historic sites. The mills of Hunterdon are preserved and showcased. The historic Red Mill is the focal point of the Red Mill Museum Village in Clinton; in Stockton, the Prallsville Mills complex is a jewel within Delaware & Raritan Canal State Park.

Other architectural masterpieces of Hunterdon's past can be found in both fields and towns. Red barns are the dominant feature of the agricultural landscape, whereas historic church steeples rise above many of the earliest settlements in the county. Shoolhouses in Oak Summit, New Hampton and Bunnvale live on as museums and libraries, and Flemington's historic Court House has been restored to vintage glory. Homeowners in Hunterdon's numerous historic districts proudly maintain their vernacular farmhouses and Victorian-era mansions.

I am personally drawn to the numerous waterways of Hunterdon. The Ken Lockwood Gorge, Teetertown Ravine and the Wickecheoke Greenway are some of my favorite locations for rugged natural beauty. Devil's Tea Table offered me an awesome view of the Delaware River and its islands. As I approached the edge of the cliff, I startled a pair of red-tailed hawks that took flight and soared down below me. The county's larger waters are popular with recreational appeal, but I prefer them at quieter times—the sunrise over Spruce Run Reservoir and the moonrise over Round Valley Reservoir.

My researching and reading various websites and publications about the county's history gave me a greater understanding and appreciation of Hunterdon. This book presents the county through an alphabetical travelogue of the municipalities. At the beginning of each section I included a brief community profile with historical information distilled from my readings.

My passion and love for Hunterdon County has only grown from this experience and I hope you will enjoy and share my vision through the more than four hundred photos presented in **HUNTERDON, A Celebration of Communities**.

Alexandria
Township

In 1744, James Alexander, Scottish immigrant and Surveyor-General of New York and New Jersey, purchased 10,000 acres of land from the West Jersey Society in Bethlehem Township. By 1765, his land and other parcels were partitioned from Bethlehem Township to become Alexandria and named in his honor. Eventually Kingwood and Holland Townships were further subdivided from Alexandria. Alexandria Township has been an agrarian community for almost three centuries. Horse, dairy and crop farming continue today as vast fields cover the gently rolling countryside of the Hunterdon Plateau.

▲▲ ▲ *Mount Salem Church (ca. 1864), property of Alexandria Historical Society, Bloomsbury-Pittstown Road*

▲ *Prevost Farm House, library and museum of Alexandria Historical Society, Milford-Frenchtown Road*

◀ ▶ *Everittstown-Pittstown Road*

St. Thomas Episcopal Church, Sky Manor Road

▲ Palumbo's Nursery at Perrine's, Little York

▶ Pittstown Inn (ca. 1760)

▲ Mount Pleasant

▲ *Everittstown*

◀ *Senator Stout Road*

ALEXANDRIA ∞ *12* ∞ Township

Horse farm, Everittstown-Pittstown Road

Bethlehem

Township

In the northwest corner of Hunterdon, Bethlehem Township was formed in 1730. At that time Bethlehem was a much larger tract of land which included today's Alexandria, Holland, Kingwood, Union and Franklin Townships. Incorporated in 1798, Bethlehem Township is bordered by the Musconetcong Mountain—part of the New Jersey Highlands, and the beautiful Musconetcong River Valley which slopes down to its border along the river. The mineral-rich mountain gave the township its mining history which flourished from the mid-19th through early 20th centuries. The lush river valley, which attracted early settlers from Holland, is still covered with numerous farms.

▲ West Portal

▼ Mine Road

▲ ▶ Huczko Memorial Fields, Heritage Park

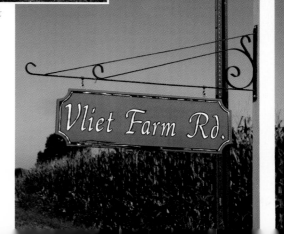

Valley Station Road

Central Valley Farm
ORGANIC
CSA
SHARES AVAILABLE

▲ *Charlestown Road*

▲ *Norton Church Road*

▲ ▶ *Tower Hill Reserve, Mountain View Road*

West Portal

▼ *Iron Bridge Road*

▲ *Hackett Road*

▶ *West Portal-Asbury Road*

▶ *Mine Road*

▶ *Blackbrook Road*

H&H Farms
174 Blackbrook Road

Bloomsbury
Borough

Bloomsbury, a quaint village located on the south side of the Musconetcong River, was originally part of Bethlehem Township and was incorporated in 1905. Named for the Bloom Family, the borough's industrial past featured an iron works that processed ore mined from the nearby Musconetcong Mountain. Located in the northwestern corner of the county bordering Warren County, Bloomsbury is now a quiet residential community with tree-lined streets and front porches decorated with flags and flowers.

▼ *Main Street*

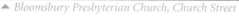

▲ *North Street*

▲ *Bloomsbury Presbyterian Church, Church Street*

▲ *Bloomsbury Elementary School, Main Street*

Musconetcong River spillway near Bloomsbury Bridge

BLOOMSBURY ❖❖❖ *21* ❖❖❖ Borough

▲ *Center Street*

▲ *Main Street*

War Memorial, Main Street

Califon
Borough

Small-town America can still be found on the banks of the South Branch Raritan River. An early mill site and train stop on the High Bridge Railroad, Califon was originally named "California" by miller Jacob Neighbors in celebration of "Gold Fever" which swept the nation in the mid-1800s. The name was eventually shortened and the borough was officially carved from neighboring Lebanon and Tewksbury Townships in 1918. The Califon National Historic District is comprised of over 150 structures giving this quaint village its Victorian-era charm.

▼ *Borough of Califon Municipal Offices*

▼ *The Station at Califon, museum of Califon Historical Society*

▲ *Califon Bridge decorated for Memorial Day*

Califon Bridge over South Branch Raritan River

Abraham Philhower's
General Store
~1888~

Presented by
Califon Historical Society

| John Beavers circa 1890 | J.B. Apgar 1905-1916 |
| J.B. and LM.Apgar 1916-1929 | LM.Apgar 1929-1951 |

| Howard Bartles 1951-1952 | Irma and Leonard Rambo 1952 - 1980 |
| d Rambo ons 0-1998 | Donald and Marie Freibergs 1998 - |

*Califon National Historic District,
Main Street*

Dr. Theodore Miller
"House   Pharmacy"
Circa 1881   Circa 1900
CALIFON HISTORICAL SOCIETY

▲ *Memorial Day Parade*

◀ ▼ *Califon Firemen's Fair*

▼ *Califon Island Park*

Clinton
Town

In the 1750s a dam and mill were built on the South Branch Raritan River just below the entrance to Spruce Run. With a tavern, mills and quarry the location became important during the Revolution and was the site of New Jersey's first "Minutemen." In 1782 Daniel Hunt purchased the mill site, thus the community surrounding the mills became known as Hunt's Mills. By the early 19th century it was renamed Clinton, in honor of New York Governor DeWitt Clinton, proponent of the Erie Canal. The Great Fire in 1891 brought devastation to Main Street, but was followed by a period of rebuilding in the Victorian style that survives today. Prosperity followed through the 20th century as the town grew and the mills evolved into cultural centers showcasing art and history. Today shops and restaurants complete Clinton's transition into a popular tourist locale.

▼ *Red Mill, South Branch Raritan River*

▼ *Red Mill Museum Village*

◄ *Main Street*   ▲ *Clinton Municipal Building, Leigh Street*

Red Mill (ca. 1810), view from West Main Street Bridge (1870)

◀ ▼ Hunterdon Chamber of Commerce
"Taste of Clinton" event, Main Street

◀ Shakespeare Summer Festival

▼ Dickens Days

▼ Shakespeare Summer Festival

GUYS WANTED, DAMES in NEED of help!

▲ Shakespeare
Summer Festival
Parade

◀ ▶

Revolutionary
War Days, Red Mill
Museum Village

Hunterdon Museum of Art,
housed in the Stone Mill (1836)

Canoeing on the South Branch Raritan River

Clinton
Township

The Lower Minisink Trail was an early Lenape path which connected the Raritan and Delaware Rivers. European settlers followed this pathway and built farms and mills near Hunt's Mills, Lebanon and Beaver Brook. The trail evolved into the Easton-Brunswick Road (chartered as the New Jersey Turnpike). Early in the 20th century, it was paved and renamed U.S. Highway 22. A north-south branch of this trail became Spruce Run Turnpike, today's U.S. Highway 31. Clinton Township was partitioned from Lebanon Township in 1841 and remained a quiet farming area through the early 20th century. A natural "round valley" nestled within Cushetunk Mountain was dammed in the 1960s to become a vital reservoir and popular recreation area.

Round Valley Reservoir

▼ *Old Mountain Road*

Round Valley Reservoir

▲ Gray Rock Road

▼ *Allerton United Methodist Church, Allerton Road*

▲ *Valley Brook Farm, U.S. Route 22*

▲ *Cokesbury Road*

◀ ▼ *Stanton Mountain Road*

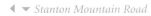

Deats Gazebo (1893), Hunterdon Arboretum

▲ *North Hunterdon High School Commencement*

▲ *Immaculate Conception Parish Festival*

▶ *Blueberry Festival & Dinner,*
Stanton Community Grange #148

Bass Lane

Delaware
Township

A farming area since the early 1700s, Delaware Township lies in the southwestern portion of the county and was carved from Amwell Township in 1838. The rocky Lockatong and Wickecheoke Creeks wind through the township en route to the Delaware and Raritan Canal and the Delaware River on the township's western border. These waterways are traversed by historic bridges and are bordered by acres of preserves and greenways. Charming historic hamlets like Sergeantsville, Rosemont, Sandy Ridge, Raven Rock and Locktown complement the stone farmhouses and magnificent barns of Delaware's pastoral countryside.

▼ *Wickecheoke Greenway, Lower Ferry Road*

▲ *Locktown Baptist Church*

▲ *Green Sergeant's Covered Bridge*

Driving Show,
Delaware Valley
Horsemen's Association,
Route 604

▲ Sergeantsville Farmers Market

▼ Curtis Leeds, host of "Rock House,"
WDVR studio, Sergeantsville

▲ Sergeantsville General Store

▼ Orchard Hill Farm, Sergeantsville

Headquarters Farm,
Zentek Road

▲ Rosemont-Ringoes Road

▲ Wescott Nature Preserve, Raven Rock-Rosemont Road

▼ Locktown

▶ Laura T. Barnes,
children's book author,
Sergeantsville

▲ *Civil War encampment, Holcombe-Jimison Farmstead Museum, Daniel Bray Highway*
▶ *Bull's Island, Delaware & Raritan Canal State Park, Daniel Bray Highway*

Delaware & Raritan Canal State Park

East Amwell
Township

Established by Royal Patent from Queen Anne in 1708, Amwell Township was a vast tract which encompassed almost half of today's Hunterdon County. East Amwell was partitioned from this territory in 1846 and borders Somerset and Mercer Counties on the southeastern corner of the county. The Sourland Mountain slopes northwesterly into the wide and fertile Amwell Valley where farming and open space prevail. Hunterdon's oldest settlement of Ringoes, along with the hamlets of Weert's Corner, Larison's Corner and parts of Reaville, give small town character to this rural township.

▼ *East Amwell Elementary School*

▼ *Wertsville*

▼ *Amwell Lake*

▼ *Harvest Moon Inn, former Amwell Academy (1811), Ringoes*

▲ *"Highfields,"*
Charles Lindbergh Estate

Wertsville Road

Lindbergh Road

▶ *Amwell Road*

Hunterdon County
4H & Agricultural Fair,
County Fairgrounds,
South County Park

▲ ▼ *Unionville Vineyards*

▲ *Simon Boyar entertains at Unionville Vineyards*

▼ *Amwell Valley Vineyard*

▼ Bob Rowe

TICKETS

BLACK RIVER

TO TRAINS
TRACK 1

752

GIFT SHOP

▲ Black River & Western Railroad, Ringoes Station

◀ Bob Rowe's roadside train display, Toad Lane

▲ Frontage Road

◀ ▲ *Candlelight Farm, Reaville*

◀ ▼ *Wertsville Road*

*Fawn Run Farm,
Wertsville Road*

*Hunterdon County Chamber of Commerce,
"Hunterdon Horse Expo," County Fairgrounds, South County Park*

Flemington
Borough

Flemington was originally part of a land parcel owned by William Penn and Daniel Coxe. Colonists settled in the area in the 1730s. Samuel Fleming purchased some land and built a tavern in 1756—the first of "Fleming's Town." Flemington became the County Seat in 1785 and through the early and mid-19th century its Main Street flourished with the addition of a court house, hotel and other grand buildings built in Greek Revival and Victorian style. In 1935, Flemington's court house was host to the Lindbergh "trial of the century." Flemington is equally famous for its pottery, glass, furs and factory outlets. Today, Main Street is alive and bustling with restaurants and events which celebrate this historic setting.

▲ ▶ *Historic Hunterdon County Court House*

▼ *Hunterdon County Justice Center*

▼ *Stangl Pottery Museum at Pfaltzgraff Outlet*

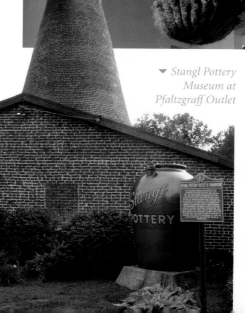

Union Hotel, Main Street

Flemington Borough Park

▲ *Doric House, Main Street*

◀ *War Memorial, Main Street*

Fleming Castle, Bonnell Street

FLEMING CASTLE,
THE FIRST HOUSE
IN THE VILLAGE,
BUILT BY SAMUEL FLEMING
1756.

THIS TABLET IS ERECTED BY
COLONEL LOWREY CHAPTER
DAUGHTERS OF THE
AMERICAN REVOLUTION,
MAY 23, 1906.

▼ Main Street

▼ Pennsylvania Avenue

▲ East Main Street

▲ Flemington Traffic Circle

▼ Liberty Village

▲ Turntable Junction

▼ Black River & Western Railroad and Feed Mill Plaza

Franklin
Township

Located near the geographic center of Hunterdon, Franklin Township straddles the Capoolong Creek—a scenic tributary of the South Branch Raritan River which flows down from the Hunterdon Plateau. English and Quaker settlers arrived here in the early 18th century; however, it wasn't until 1845 that Franklin was created from Kingwood Township. Peach farms dominated the area into the late 1800s when Franklin was the "Peach Capital" of New Jersey—and possibly the whole country. The Pittstown Branch Railroad was built to facilitate the export of the crop. Franklin's rural charm is evident today in its numerous farms, mills and villages.

▼ *Pittstown Mill (Hoff's Mill, 1760)*

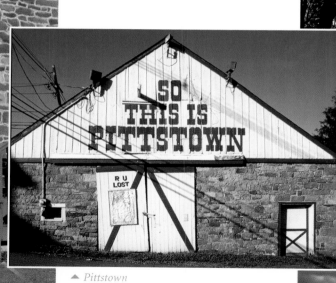

▲ *Friends Meeting House, Quakertown*

▼ *Cherryville*

▲ *Pittstown*

White Bridge Road over Capoolong Creek

▲ Peterson Farm, Cherryville Road

▲ ▶ Strawberry Festival,
Cherryville Baptist Church

▲ Quakertown

▲ Locust Grove Road

▼ River Road

◀ Toshiko Takaezu,
nationally renowned
artist of clay vessels

▲ Kiceniuk Road bridge

Leon's SOD FARMS
WHOLESALE / RETAIL
713-9496

Site of
Oak Grove Grange # 119
Chartered June 30, 1896
Charter surrendered 1988
Original building built in 1898
on land owned by H.K.Wright.
Grange founded for purpose of cooperative
buying to lower costs for farmers.

▲ *Oak Grove Grange, Pittstown Road*

CPS SEED
4022RRCBCRW

CPS SEED
4042RRCBCRW

CPS SEED

▲ *Locust Grove Road*

◀ *Clifford E. and Melda C. Snyder*
Research and Extension Farm,
Center for Sustainable Agriculture,
Cook College, Rutgers University,
Locust Grove Road

FARM STAND 400 ft
OPEN
Corn

▲ *Quakertown*

White Bridge Road

River Road

Kingtown Road

Quakertown Road

Spring Hill Road

Frenchtown
Borough

Archaeological evidence reveals that the Lenape people inhabited "Nishisakawick" for thousands of years before a mill and ferry crossing were established there in the 1730s. James Alexander was the original owner of the area, and his son, William, surveyed and planned a village at this site. In 1776 Colonel Thomas Lowrey purchased the land and later sold it to Paul Henri Mallet, a Swiss writer who fled the French Revolution in 1794. "French Town" was named for the new French-speaking owner. A wooden bridge was built across the Delaware River in 1841 connecting Frenchtown to Pennsylvania and soon afterward the Belvidere-Delaware Railroad connected it to river towns north and south. Both pathways led to a period of robust growth. Frenchtown remains a charming river town that celebrates "Bastille Day" in honor of its namesake.

▼ Borough Hall, Second Street

▶ *Frenchtown band, "The Common Ground" performing at Bastille Day celebration*

▼ *Book Garden, Bridge Street*

▲ Painted mule and mural, Harrison Street

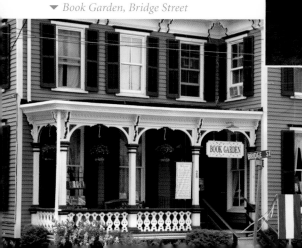

Frenchtown-Tinicum Bridge, Delaware River

The National Hotel, Race Street   ▶ *Harrison Street*

▶ *Bridge Street*

▶ *Race Street*

Girl Scout Troop 1189 in Memorial Day Parade

Memorial Day Parade

Keaton getting a trim, Schaible's Barber Shop, Race Street

Glen Gardner
Borough

In the early 1700s colonists migrated westward along the Lenape pathways; some settled in a small "glen" along Spuce Run. John Eveland established a tavern in 1760 and the settlement became known as Eveland's Tavern. In 1820 John Clark opened a store which housed the post office and the name was then changed to Clarksville. The mid-19th century was a time of growth and prosperity when the Central Railroad of New Jersey arrived. In 1863 the Gardner brothers moved from New York City and started a manufacturing business that grew to employ 700 people. The town was renamed Glen Gardner and was incorporated as a Borough in 1919. Industry departed and Glen Gardner is now a quiet residential community.

▼ *Municipal Building*

▼ *Main Street*

◀ ▲ *Grochowicz Farms, U.S. Route 31*

GROCHOWICZ FARMS
(908) 537-6130
EST. 1952

School Street Bridge (1867) over Spruce Run Creek

▲ *Glen Gardner Inn (1760)*

▼ *Main Street*

▲ *Hot Rod's Hot Dogs, U.S. Route 31*

▼ *Bridge, Main Street*

BUILT
BY
A.S. BANGHART
1875

J. HIPP

▲ Glen Gardner General Store

▼ Hill Road Bridge

▼ Fountain Grove Cemetery

GLEN GARDNER ⁌ 77 ⁌ Borough

Hampton
Borough

Hampton, a small village on the Musconetcong River, was named after Jonathan Hampton who donated land for a local church. The borough experienced most of its growth in the mid-1800s from the expansion of railroads. Nestled between Bethelehem and Lebanon Townships on the northwestern border of the county, the town was once known as "Junction" because it was located at the convergence of the Jersey Central Railroad with the Delaware, Lackawanna and Western Railroad—making the connection to Pennsylvania's rich anthracite coal fields. The railroads are now no longer active and Hampton is a quiet residential community with Victorian-era homes on tree-lined streets.

▼ *Musconetcong Valley Presbyterian Church*

▲ *Valley Road*

▲ *Borough Hall*
▶ *Veterans Park*

▲ *New Street*

Railroad Bridge over Main Street

Main Street

St. Ann's Roman Catholic Church, Church Street

High Bridge
Borough

The Lenape people lived in this area for thousands of years before European settlers arrived around 1700. Philadelphia businessmen Allen and Turner leased a tract of land from the West Jersey Society which included today's High Bridge and they started the Union Forge Ironworks. Robert Taylor, an Irish immigrant, joined the company as a bookkeeper and eventually was promoted to Supervisor. An ardent Patriot, Taylor supplied cannon balls for the American Revolution. After the war he purchased the forge, which eventually became known as Taylor-Wharton and operated until the 1960s. In the mid 1800s the Jersey Central Railroad constructed a "high bridge" across the South Branch Raritan River. High Bridge Township was formed in 1871 and was further subdivided in 1898 to become High Bridge Borough. Today, High Bridge is a vibrant town with numerous community events.

▼ *Solitude House Museum*

▲ *Double-arched culvert (1859) replaced the original "high bridge" over South Branch Raritan River*

◀ *Site of Taylor-Wharton Ironworks*

High Bridge Dam

Taylor Street

High Bridge Reformed Church,
Church Street

▲ Arch Street

▶ North Hunterdon
Little League,
Union Forge Park

Within the collage, the following text appears on a sign:

POOCH 6/17
PARADE → 8:45

Annual "Pooch Parade" at High Bridge Commons

Holland
Township

The northwestern corner of Alexandria Township was slowly settled during the 18th and 19th centuries. By the 1870s residents succeeded in a second attempt to break away from Alexandria to become its own municipality—Holland Township. Bordered by the Musconetcong and Delaware Rivers, Holland straddles Riegel Ridge of the New Jersey Highlands where forests and farms are still commonplace in this sparsely populated corner of the county. The Volendam Windmill Museum, a replica of a wind-driven Dutch mill was built in the 1960s by the late Paul Jorgenson and is a tribute to the early settlers.

▼ *Volendam Windmilll Museum*

VOLENDAM WINDMILL

AUTHENTIC REPLICA OF WIND-DRIVEN MILL USED FOR GRINDING GRAIN INTO FLOUR.

▲ *Stamets Road*

▲ *Pursley's Ferry Historic District*

◄ *Late Triassic strata, Milford Cliffs, River Road*

▲ Irises, Old River Road

▶ Delaware River, Old River Road

▲ Columbine, Riegelsville-Milford Road

▲ *Milford-Warren Glen Road*

◀ *Philips Road*

▲ *Oak Hill Golf Club*

◀ ▲ ▶
Riegel Ridge
Community Center

RIEGEL
RIDGE
COMMUNITY
CENTER

BETHANY RIDGE

Holland Presbyterian Church (1849), Church and Riegelsville Roads

Kingwood
Township

Partitioned from Bethlehem Township in 1746, Kingwood Township's present borders were finalized in the mid-1800s when Franklin and Frenchtown were later separated from it. Early settlements included Kingwood Village, Tumble, Milltown (Idell), Baptistown and Barbertown. The Hunterdon Plateau drops steeply to meet the Delaware River on Kingwood's western border. Warford Rock, a natural formation also known as "Devil's Tea Table," is perched high above the river near Tumble Falls overlooking some islands in the Delaware that are also part of the township. Kingwood remains rural with farms and hamlets and it is the least densely populated municipality within the county.

▶ *Warford Rock ("Devil's Tea Table")*

▲ *Tubing on the Delaware River*

▼ *Kingwood Road*

▲ *Salzberg's Eggs, Route 12*

Delaware River, view from "Devil's Tea Table"

*Farm scenes near
Union and
Kingwood Roads*

▼ *Oak Summit School (1849)*

▲ *Old Stone Meeting House (1754), currently home to
First Unitarian Universalist Fellowship of Hunterdon County*

▼ *Warsaw Road*

OAK SUMMIT
SCHOOL

ERECTED IN 1849 AT A COST
OF $400. USED ALMOST
CONTINUOUSLY UNTIL 1953.
ACCOMMODATED UP TO 40
STUDENTS WITH ONE TEACHER.

◄ WDVR's "Heartlands Hayride,"
broadcast from Kingwood Township
Fire Company Banquet Hall, Baptistown

◄ ▲ "OPA! Big 'Fat' Greek Festival,"
(at Razberry's, U.S. Route 12),
The Greek Orthodox Parish of Hunterdon

Lambertville

City

As Hunterdon's only city, Lambertville may be small in size, but it is certainly cosmopolitan. John Holcombe was the first settler in 1705, and Emanuel Coryell followed in 1732 starting a ferry crossing on York Road. "Coryell's Ferry" was an important stop for travelers between New York and Philadelphia. When a new post office was built in 1810 the settlement was renamed "Lambert's Ville" honoring local resident and U.S. Senator John Lambert. Commercial and industrial growth flourished in the mid-19th century because of the Delaware & Raritan Canal's connection to Trenton and the Belvidere-Delaware Railroad's connection to the river towns north. The Lewis family operates the last and only commercial shad fishery in the state and Lambertville's annual Shad Fest celebrates the spring return of the migratory shad. Lambertville's Victorian-era mansions and industrial buildings have been transformed into *Bed & Breakfast* inns, shops and restaurants to create a lovely tourist destination.

▲ ▼ *Shad Fest 2006—Celebrating 25 years!*

▼ *Shad nets, Lewis Island*

▼ *New Hope-Lambertville (Free) Bridge*

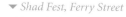
▲ *Shad Fest, Ferry Street*

Shad fishing from Lewis Island on the Delaware River

◀ *PBS Antiques Roadshow experts,*
Suzanne Perrault and David Rago,
Rago Arts and Auction Center,
North Main Street

Lambertville, aerial view

▲ Delaware & Raritan Canal State Park

▼ James Wilson Marshall House, Bridge Street

▲ Martin Coryell House (1864),
Bed & Breakfast,
North Union Street

◀ Mansion (1865),
North Union Street

Kalmia Club (1892), York Street

Lebanon

Borough

Originally a trading post and stagecoach stop along the Easton-Brunswick Road, Lebanon Borough was officially created from Clinton Township in 1926; however, church records indicate a settlement at this location from the early 1700s. Earlier names of this location include Jacksonville, Lebanonville and Lebanonville Depot after the Central Railroad of New Jersey built a station there in the 1850s. Lebanon's charming Victorian homes are festooned with flags and buntings for its annual July 4th Parade— the longest running Independence Day celebration in the county. Today Lebanon Borough is a residential community sitting in the shadow of Cushetunk Mountain and Round Valley Reservoir.

▲ *Lebanon Boro General Store, Main Street*

 ◀◀ ◀ ▼ *July 4th Baby & Bicycle Parade*

July 4th Parade, Main Street

Lebanon Railroad Station and tracks

▲ *The Dollhouse Factory, Main Street*
◀ *High Street*

Lebanon
Township

Lebanon Township, formed in 1731 and incorporated in 1798, was a larger tract of land before the subsequent subdivisions of Clinton and Tewksbury Townships and the Boroughs of Califon, High Bridge, Clinton and Glen Gardner were created from it. Lebanon Township is the county's northernmost municipality and sits at the foothills of the scenic New Jersey Highlands, along the Musconetcong and South Branch Raritan Rivers. Over half of the township remains forested with many of the acres preserved in state and county parks. The balance of the land is agricultural interspersed with the small hamlets of Bunnvale, Lower Valley, New Hampton and Woodglen.

▼ South Branch Raritan River, Ken Lockwood Gorge

▼ Teetertown Ravine Nature Preserve

▲ Musconetcong River near Point Mountain Reservation

▼ Great Blue Heron, Ken Lockwood Gorge

South Branch Raritan River, Ken Lockwood Gorge

▲ Bunnvale Library, former Bunnvale School #9 (1915)

▲ Penwell Mills (1855)

▲ *Maple Lane*

▶ *Musconetcong River,*
Lackawanna Railroad trestle,
Changewater

▼ *Teetertown*

▲ *Hickory Run Farm,*
High Bridge - Califon Road

▶ *Maple Lane*

Ashton's Farm,
High Bridge - Califon Road

Milford
Borough

Milford started as an 18th century mill site at the ford of a waterway—the Hakihokake Creek near its junction with the Delaware River. The original grist mill was destroyed by fire in 1769, and the settlement became known as "Burnt Mills." After Colonel Thomas Lowrey moved there from Frenchtown in the late 18th century, building houses and new mills, it was renamed "Lowrytown." In the early 1800s it was changed to "Millford" and by mid-century the spelling changed slightly to "Milford." A bridge across the Delaware River was built in 1842, and the arrival of the Belvidere-Delaware Railroad in 1853 brought new growth to this river town, which was incorporated as a borough in 1911. Today "Milford on the Delaware" prides itself on its hometown charm.

▼ *Upper Black Eddy-Milford Bridge*

▼ *Presbyterian Church of Milford and view of Carpenter Street*

▼ *York Street*

▼ *Spring Garden Street*

Milford, view from Valley View Avenue

▲ Longview Road

▼ Chestnut Hill on the Delaware Bed & Breakfast, Church Street

▲ Railroad Avenue

▼ Adrienne Crombie's mural on Milford Post Office, Route 519 & Bridge Street

▼ Milford Railroad Station (1853), Railroad Avenue

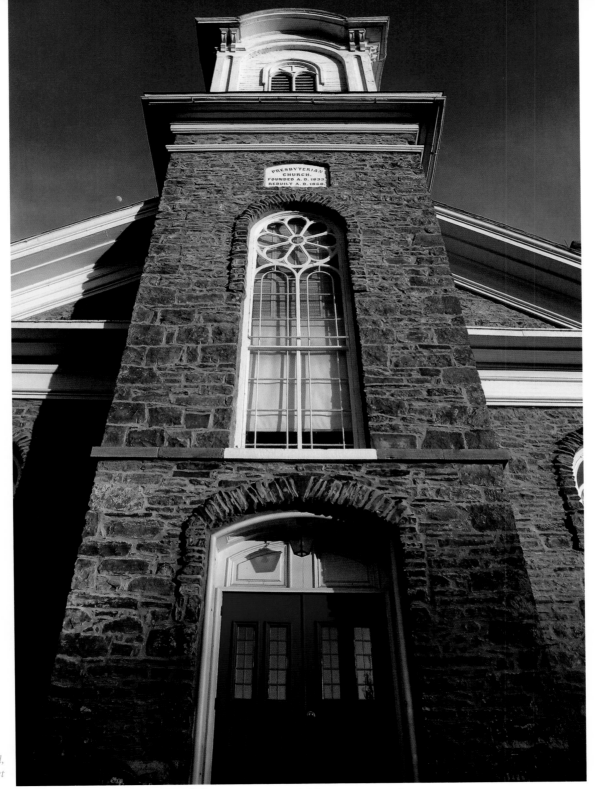

Presbyterian Church of Milford,
Bridge Street

Raritan
Township

As part of the original Amwell Township established by Queen Anne in 1708, Raritan Township was subdivided from Amwell in 1838. Taking its name from the Raritan River which forms its northeastern border, Raritan Township is the county's second largest municipality in area, and ranks first in population. It encircles the county seat of Flemington and is Hunterdon's center of commerce which developed along Highways 202 & 31 and remnants of colonial Old York Road. Raritan Township is also home to Hunterdon Medical Center. Beyond the highways and housing, Raritan's agrarian past can still be found in the numerous farms and rural villages that complement this modern community.

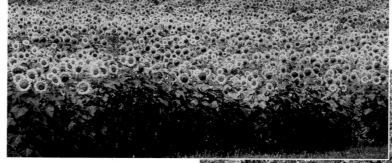

▲ *River Road*

FURSTOVER
ANTIQUES

STANTON
STATION
COUNTRY STORE

Country Gifts
Candles Cards

▲ *Furstover Antiques,
Stanton Station Road*

◀ *Stanton Station*

Dvoor Farm, U.S. Route 12 Circle

▲ *Good News Home for Women, Bartles Corner Road*

▲ *Reaville Road*

◀ *Thatcher Hill Road*

▲ *Northlandz, U.S. Route 202*

▼ *HealthQuest, U.S. Route 31*

▲ *Hunterdon Medical Center*
▶ *H.M.C. staff with dedicated volunteer, Margaret Rogers, age 94*
▼ *Volunteers, Pet Therapy Program at Hunterdon Medical Center*

▲ *Don Mattingly 17 & Under World Series at the Jack Cust Baseball Academy*

▲ *Hunterdon County Complex, U.S. Route 12*

▲ *Heron Glen Golf Course, U.S. Route 202/31*

Residential neighborhoods, aerial view

Readington
Township

Colonel John Reading, one of the first settlers of Hunterdon County, bought a large plantation which he named "Mount Amwell" after his home in England. Created by Royal Charter in 1730, "Readings" was the first township in the newly-created Hunterdon County and officially became Readington Township in 1798. Readington was the gateway for English and Dutch settlers moving westward from neighboring Somerset County. Evidence of these colonial settlements can be found along these routes at Potterstown, White House, Centerville, Stanton and Three Bridges. As the county's largest municipality in area and second most populous, Readington is a thriving community, yet it still retains much of its rural character.

▲ Stanton General Store, view from Stanton Reformed Church

▼ Readington Reformed Church

▼ Revolutionary War soldier's grave, Whitehouse Station

▼ Cub Scout Pack 61 fishing at Deer Path Park, West Woodschurch Road

Wildflowers, U.S. Route 22, Whitehouse Station

▲ Horse show at
Briarwood Farms,
Pleasant Run Road

◀ "Pony Share" offers rides at
Anderson House Seafood Festival,
Deer Path Park

▲ *New World Dutch Barn (1820),*
Bouman-Stickney Farmstead, Dreahook Road

◀ *Dart's Mill National*
Historic District, Route 523

▶ *Eversole-Hall House,*
Whitehouse Station

QuickChek
New Jersey Festival of Ballooning,
Solberg Airport

QuickChek
New Jersey Festival of Ballooning,
Solberg Airport

THIS FLAGPOLE IS
ERECTED IN FULFILLMENT OF
THE WISH OF
THOR SOLBERG
AND
DEDICATED TO HIM ON THE
50TH ANNIVERSARY OF HIS
PIONEER FLIGHT FROM
NEW YORK TO NORWAY,
JULY 19, 1985

▲ *Danielle, Dawn, Stephanie & Veronica,*
waitresses at Spinning Wheel Diner, U.S. Route 22

◀ *"Little Chamomile Man,"*
courtyard at Merck & Co. Inc.,
Whitehouse Station

▶ *Summer night at Polar Cub,*
U.S. Route 22, Whitehouse

Chef Craig Shelton, The Ryland Inn, Whitehouse

Stockton
Borough

As an early 18th century ferry crossing, this settlement was known as Reading Ferry, Howell's Ferry and Centre Bridge Station before officially being named Stockton in 1851. Named for Commodore Robert F. Stockton, president of the Delaware & Raritan Canal Company, Stockton Borough was partitioned from Delaware Township and incorporated in 1898. Stockton's growth continued through the 19th century after a bridge to Pennsylvania was built in 1814, followed by the construction of the Canal and the railroad in the mid-19th century. Stockton was home to numerous mills and quarries. With industry and railroads now gone, Stockton is Hunterdon's smallest municipality, but thriving with historic inns, restaurants and galleries.

▲ *John Prall, Jr. House, U.S. Route 29*

▼ *St. Agnes Roman Catholic Church, Main Street*

▼ *Stockton Veterans Honor Roll*

▲ *"Snowy Reflections" by Anita Shrager, painted on Bridge Street*

Prallsville Mills, Delaware & Raritan Canal State Park

▲ "Tom," The Woolverton Inn (1792)

▲ Stockton School (1832)

▲ Mural (ca. 1930)

▼ Wishing Well, made famous by Rodgers & Hart

Stockton Inn (ca. 1710)

▲ *Silver dollar in floor*

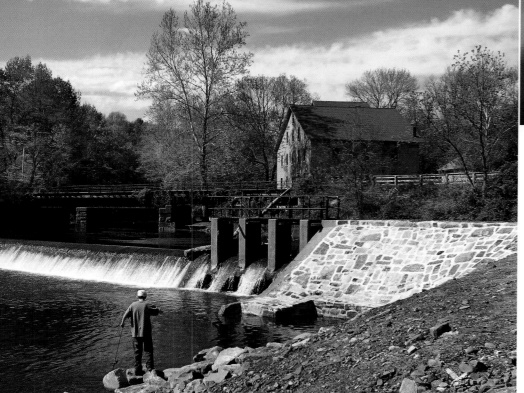

Prallsville Mills, Delaware & Raritan Canal State Park

Stockton Wesleyan Church, North Main Street

Tewksbury
Township

In 1708, George Willocks purchased a parcel of land covering the southeastern third of present day Tewksbury. Soon afterwards, the West Jersey Society purchased a larger tract of land, which bordered Willocks line and extended to the Delaware River. The first settlers of the area were predominantly from England; however, by the mid-18th century a large German population was also present. Originally part of Lebanon Township, Tewksbury was established in 1755 and was probably named after Tewkesbury, England. The early 18th century settlements of Lamington Falls, Germantown and Bull's Head are currently known as the quaint villages of Pottersville, Oldwick and Mountainville. Today, the rolling hills of Tewksbury are home to numerous horse farms, orchards and estate homes.

▼ *Oldwick Community Center & Library*

▲ ▼ *Copper Creek Farm, Wintermute Farm Lane*

▲ *Christie Hoffman Farm Park, Fairmount Road*

▼ *Pottersville Post Office*

Homestead Road

▲ ▼ *Homestead Road*

◀ ▲ *Tewksbury Education Foundation's*
11th Annnual Barn Dance and Auction

Spring flowers along Rockaway Creek, Hill and Dale Road

Melick's Town Farm, Oldwick

Walter Chandoha, photographer and garden expert, guest speaker at the Hunterdon Hills Garden Club garden tour, Snuffys Lane

The Christmas Tree Farm, Saw Mill Road

▼ Zion Lutheran Church, Oldwick

▲ Mountainville

▲ Oldwick General Store, Oldwick

▼ Boulder Hill Road

Vliettown Road

◀ *Fox Hill Road*

TEWKSBURY *148* Township

McCan Mill Road

Union
Township

Union Township was named after Union Furnace—part of Union Forge Ironworks built by Philadelphia businessmen Allen and Turner in 1742. The ironworks produced farming equipment, as well as military hardware during the American Revolution. Forests were clear-cut to feed the furnace fires, and in the process, fields were created for farming. The furnace site was covered in the early 1960s by the creation of Spruce Run Reservoir. Union Township was the southern part of Bethlehem Township and was partitioned from it in 1853. The first township meetings were held at the brick tavern in Perryville, which was named in honor of Commodore Oliver Perry's naval victory at Lake Erie during the War of 1812. Today, Union Township is bisected by U.S. Interstate 78 yet remains sparsely populated and agricultural.

▼ *Pattenburg*

◀ *Union Grandin Cemetery*

▼ *Bethlehem Presbyterian Church, Grandin*

▶ *Union Furnace Nature Preserve*

Hay field along Route 614

South Branch
Watershed Association,
"Ride for the River,"
Spruce Run State Park

▲ Spruce Run Reservoir

▲ *Perryville Inn (1812)*　　　　　▶ *David Reynolds Tavern (1783)*

▼ *Municipal Hall, Jutland*

Pittstown Road

West Amwell

Township

Amwell Township, created by Royal Patent in 1708, was named for settler John Reading's ancestral home in Amwell, England. West Amwell, the southernmost municipality in the county, was officially created from Amwell Township in 1846. Lambertville was part of the township until it broke away two years later. West Amwell's first township meeting was held in a tavern in Mount Airy—an early site previously known as Amwell Meeting. Mount Airy was later a stage stop on the Swiftsure Line. West Amwell straddles the rocky Sourland Plateau and overlooks the Delaware River. Vantage points near Goat Hill were used by General Washington during the Revolution. West Amwell remains a picturesque rural farming community.

▼ United Water Lambertville Reservoir

▲ Route 179

▲ Rocktown-Lambertville Road

▶ Wildflowers, Rock Road

Mount Airy

▲ George Washington Road

▲ Amwell Methodist Episcopal "Old Rocks" Church (1843)

▼ ▶ Golden Nugget Antique Flea Market, U.S. Route 29

▼ Mount Airy

Chimney Hill Estate (1820), Goat Hill Road

▲ Lambertville
Iris Patch,
Brunswick Pike

◀ South Hunterdon
Regional High School
Marching Band

Grand Army of the Republic Monument (1900),
South Hunterdon Regional High School

HUNTERDON MEDICAL CENTER

Acknowledged as a leader in developing comprehensive medical and health care services,
Hunterdon Medical Center is a 178-bed non-profit community hospital. Our goal is
to meet the needs with health care that is compassionate and effective.
We provide a full range of preventive, diagnostic and therapeutic
inpatient and outpatient hospital and community health services.

Our staff is committed to providing the highest quality care to our patients.
The Hunterdon Medical Center is also a teaching institution and is affiliated with
the University of Medicine and Dentistry of New Jersey—Robert Wood Johnson Medical School.

The Family Practice Residency Program is one of the first in the nation
for the training of specialists in family medicine. Hunterdon Medical Center
is licensed by the New Jersey Department of Health, and accredited
by the Joint Commission on Accreditation of Healthcare Organizations (JCAHO).

Hunterdon County Chamber of Commerce

Hunterdon County Chamber of Commerce is an action-oriented business organization
that promotes a favorable business climate for its membership and community;
works with other interested organizations to develop effective mechanisms
for taking action on issues of community interest; and provides business leadership
for improvement of the economy and quality of life in Hunterdon County.

Weichert Realtors - Clinton Office

*As Hunterdon's leading real estate office, we are a proud sponsor of this
wonderful endeavor which celebrates the vibrancy of our communities
and showcases the incredible beauty of our county.*

Califon Historical Society
Califon

Hunterdon Hills Garden Club
Clinton

Ron & Martha Subber / The Private Advisor, Inc.
Clinton

Tewksbury Education Foundation
Tewksbury

Laura & Jefferson Barnes Sergeantsville	**Huggables Hallmark** Whitehouse Station
Bob & Pamela Beatty Clinton	**Hunterdon Musical Instrument** Flemington
Book Garden Frenchtown	**Patricia Lillis** Flemington
Califon Book Shop Califon	**Oldwick General Store** Oldwick
Clinton Book Shop Clinton	**Tewksbury Historical Society** Tewksbury
Delaware Valley Horsemen's Association Sergeantsville	**Kenneth & Janet Tremaine** Milford

Stuart & Wendy Ashton
Phyllis R. Black
Dr. & Mrs. Kenneth Cummings
Jonathan K. Horiuchi & Alice M. Kee
Robert & Sandra Rowe
The Szczepanski Family
Susan & Ronald Warrick

WALTER CHOROSZEWSKI

*For over 25 years, Walter Choroszewski has been promoting a positive image of New Jersey through his photographic creativity. He has self-published numerous regional wall calendars and coffee-table books. Among his previous New Jersey books are **LAMBERTVILLE** and **HUNTERDON COUNTY, A Millennial Portrait**. Walter enjoys speaking to various groups and he encourages elementary school children to take pride in New Jersey through his popular school presentations. Walter and his wife, Susan, live in the quaint village of South Branch in Somerset County.*

SOURCES & ACKNOWLEDGEMENTS

I am not a historian nor expert on Hunterdon County, thus my Foreword and community profiles are based on the writings of many other individuals. I wish to thank them for their invaluable contributions which aided me in this publication. My research was accomplished through internet-based resources. Every effort has been made to include all reference sources; however, there is a chance that errors and omissions may have occurred. I apologize to any parties I have omitted and will gladly credit them in future editions.

My primary source of information was the County of Hunterdon website, www.co.hunterdon.nj.us, which published an online version of the Hunterdon County Cultural & Heritage Commission publication: **The First 275 Years of Hunterdon County, 1714-1989**: **History of Hunterdon County from inception to 1989** by Dr. Hubert G. Schmidt. Also useful from the county website were the sections from the Department of Parks and Recreation and the Municipalities of the County of Hunterdon, with respective links to each municipality maintaining their own website.

These municipality websites included: www.alexandria-nj.us; www.califon.org; www.clintonnj.gov (history by Frank A. Curcio); www.eastamwelltownship.com; www.ci.flemington.nj.us; www.frenchtown.com; www.highbridge.org; www.kingwood.hunterdon.nj.us (excerpts from **Kingwood Township of Yesteryear** by Barbara & Alexander Farnham); www.lambertvillenj.org; www.lebanonboro.com (subtopics: **The Dawn of Hunterdon** by Norman C. Wittwer, **Hunterdon County Government** by Kenneth V. Myers, **Hunterdon County Transportation** by Mrs. Frederick Stothoff, **Hunterdon Transportation**, 1989 Update by John Kellogg, **Hunterdon Agriculture** by Bernard F. Ramsburg, **The Changing Face of Agriculture,** 1989 Update by George Conard, **Hunterdon Communications** by Mrs. Frederick Stothoff, **Hunterdon Communications,** 1989 Update by Edward J. Mack, **Hunterdon Industry** by Bernard F. Ramsburg, **Hunterdon Industry,** 1989 Update by Jay Comeforo); www.lebanontownship.net; www.milfordnj.org; www.raritan-township.com; www.readingtontwp.org (excerpts from **READINGTON TOWNSHIP HISTORY** by Stephanie B. Stevens); www.co.hunterdon.nj.us/mun/stockton/history.htm (excerpts from **Stockton, New Jersey: 300 Years of History** by Iris H. Naylor); www.tewksburytwp.net (history by Shaun C. Van Doren -Tewksbury Township Historian); www.westamwelltwp.org (**West Amwell Township: A Brief Early History** by Henrietta Van Syckle and Emily Nordfeldt, ca. 1975, and **Land and Natural Resources of West Amwell** by Fred Bowers, Ph.D).

Other internet resources included: www.accessgenealogy.com (Hunter Family History); www.areaguidebook.com (**Off The Beaten Path In Hunterdon** by Victoria Memminger; www.combs-families.org ("**A Gazetter of the State of New Jersey comprehending counties, town, villages, canals, rail road, &c.**" by Thomas F. Gordon, 1834); www.daytripsandrivertowns.com; www.frenchtowner.com; www.hunterdon-chamber.org; www.njskylands.com; www.njstatelib.org (**THE GOVERNORS OF NEW JERSEY 1664-1974: BIOGRAPHICAL ESSAYS,** New Jersey Historical Commission, Trenton, NJ, 1982, Paul A. Stellhorn and Michael J. Birkner, Editors); www.tewksburyhistory.net; www.westjersey.org; www.en.wikipedia.org.

On a personal level, I would like to express my sincere gratitude and appreciation to the many people who have assisted me in this endeavor. First and foremost, I would like to thank my wife and business partner, Susan Choroszewski, for her overall devotion to the project and her total involvement in almost every aspect of its production. Special thanks also goes to Debbie Lavell, our office manager who kept things running smoothly while I was lost in the creative process. I am also grateful to Robert Wise, President and CEO of Hunterdon Healthcare System for his support of this project (*and also for his great golf swing featured on p.126*); G. Meredith Betz, COO of the Hunterdon Medical Center Foundation, who graciously accepted the challenge of overseeing the fund-raiser; Kathleen Seelig, Public Relations Specialist, my liaison who coordinated the press releases; Leon Palmer, Webmaster, who maintained HMCF's internet campaign and Maria DeLuca, the kind voice at the Foundation office who fielded the advance orders for the fund-raiser. I also would like to recognize the efforts of Suzanne Lagay, President of the Hunterdon County Chamber of Commerce, for her enthusiastic support of the HMCF fund-raiser, promoting it through Chamber communications and publications.